THE ADVENTURES OF ODYSSEUS

THE ADVENTURES
OF ODYSSEUS

GERALDINE McCAUGHREAN

ILLUSTRATED BY TONY ROSS

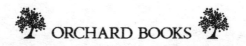

ORCHARD BOOKS

For Thomas

ORCHARD BOOKS
96 Leonard Street, London EC2A 4RH
Orchard Books Australia
14 Mars Road, Lane Cove, NSW 2066
ISBN 1 86039 434 5 (hardback)
ISBN 1 86039 526 0 (paperback)
First published in Great Britain 1997
Text © Geraldine McCaughrean 1992
Illustrations © Tony Ross 1997
1 2 3 4 5 6 02 01 00 99 98 97
The right of Geraldine McCaughrean to be identified as the
author and Tony Ross as the illustrator of this
work has been asserted by them in accordance with the
Copyright, Designs and Patents Act, 1988.
A CIP catalogue record for this book is available from the
British Library.
Printed in Great Britain

The war was over at last. At last, after
ten long years, the soldiers who had
fought in it could sail home. Among
them was Odysseus, King of Ithaca. He
and his men rowed out to sea on their
ship the *Odyssey*, leaving the battle-
fields far behind them.

There was little room aboard for food and water, but some huge jugs of wine stood in the prow, taken from the defeated enemy. Unfortunately, the first time they tasted it, the men fell asleep over their oars. "A bit too strong," decided Odysseus, watching them snore. Then a storm overtook them and blew them off course – to an island, who knows where?

Odysseus pointed up at a cliff. "I'm sure those caves up there are inhabited. Let's climb up and ask for directions and a bite to eat. Leave your swords here, and bring a jug of wine, to show we're friendly."

The first cave they came to was huge
and smelled of cheese. But nobody was
in. A fire burned in one corner. The
soldiers sat down and waited. Soon
there was a clatter of hoofs on the cliff
path, as the island shepherd drove his
flock home from the fields to the caves.
And what sheep entered the cave! They
were as big as cows, with fleeces like
snowdrifts.

But the shepherd made his sheep look tiny. He was as big as the wooden horse of Troy, and his hair hung down like creepers. A single eye winked in the centre of his forehead. He rolled a massive boulder across the cave mouth, then turned and saw his visitors.

"Supper!" he roared, in delight. And picking up a man in each paw, he gobbled them down and spat out their belts and sandals.

"Sir! We came to you in peace! How dare you eat my men!" cried Odysseus, more angry than afraid.

"I'm Polyphemus the Cyclops," said the one-eyed giant. "I eat who I want. Who are you?"

11

"I am O ... I am called No One –
and I demand that you let us go!
Why ever did I bring a present to a
man like you?"

"Present? Where? Give it! I won't eat
you if you give me a present!"

Odysseus pointed
out the jug of
wine.

Polyphemus
chewed off the
seal and gulped
down the wine.
He smacked his
lips. "Good stuff,
No One. Good
stuff."

"So you'll roll back the boulder and let us go?"

"Oh, I wouldn't shay that," slurred the Cyclops, reeling about. "What I meant to shay wash, I won't eat you ... till morning." And hooting with drunken laughter, he crashed down on his back, fast asleep.

Twelve men pushed against the boulder, but they could not roll it aside.

"We're finished, captain!" they cried.

But Odysseus was busy with the huge shepherd's crook – sharpening the end to a point with his knife. The work took all night.

Towards dawn, the sailors heated the point red-hot in the fire, lifted it to their shoulder ... and charged! They plunged the crook into the Cyclops' one horrible eye.

Polyphemus woke with a scream that brought his fellow giants running. "Polyphemus, what's wrong? Is there someone in there with you?"

"No One's in here with me!" groaned Polyphemus.

"Are you hurt, then?"

15

"No One has hurt me!" bellowed
Polyphemus.

"Good, good," said the giants
outside, and plodded back to their
caves. "Perhaps he had a nightmare,"
they said.

Polyphemus groped about blindly.
"Trickery won't save you, No One.
You and your men shan't leave this
cave alive!"

In the morning he rolled the boulder aside, so that his sheep could run out to the fields and feed. But he himself sat in the doorway, his hands spread to catch any Greek trying to escape.

Quickly, Odysseus told his men to cling on under the huge, woolly sheep, and although Polyphemus stroked each fleece as it came by him, he did not feel the man hanging on underneath.

So captain and crew escaped. But Odysseus called out as his ship sped past the cliff: "Know this, Polyphemus! It was I the hero Odysseus, who blinded you! Remember the name!"

The Cyclops picked up boulders and hurled them down, hoping to sink the little boat. "Remember it? Know this, Odysseus! I am Polyphemus, son of

Poseidon the sea god. And I call on my
father to destroy you!"

Deep in the Ocean, Poseidon heard
his son's voice, and his angry storms
drove the *Odyssey* even further off
course – to a beautiful island carpeted
with flowers.

A house stood at the top of the

beach. The crew of the Odyssey ran up
to it, and a woman welcomed them
inside. But for some reason, Odysseus
hung back. Only after the door was
shut did he peep in at the window.

The woman brought each sailor
bread, honey and wine. She carried a
golden wand, and as she circled the

table she rubbed it across their heads.

One by one, the men began to change. Their faces grew whiskery, their noses flat. They dropped the bowls, for their hands were changing into bony hoofs. One by one they rolled out of their chairs ... because pigs cannot easily sit up to table.

Pigs! Circe the enchantress had
turned them into pigs! Now she drove
them out of the back door and into her
sties, where many other pigs squealed
miserably.

Outside Odysseus searched among
the flowers at his feet. He stooped
down to pick one particular tiny white

flower, put it into his mouth, then went boldly up to the house.

"Come in! So happy to see you!" Circe's voice was as sweet as her face. She brought Odysseus bread, honey and wine. He ate the bread and honey and drank the wine. Then Circe came and stood behind him and rapped him with her golden wand. "Now get to the sty with the rest of the pigs."

"Did you know," said Odysseus, calmly taking a tangle of petals out of his mouth, "that this flower is proof against magic potions?"

Circe struck him again. But she saw that her charms were powerless.

"Odysseus!" she said. (She knew his name: that startled him.) "A fortune-teller once foretold that I would be out-tricked by one Odysseus, King of Ithaca. You are my fate! I lay my magic and my heart at your feet."

"Just turn those pigs back into men," said Odysseus.

Circe ran and thrust her golden wand into each pig's pink ear, and in moments the yard was crowded with

shivering men on hands and knees.

"Now will you love me?" Circe
begged.

"My wife, Penelope, is waiting for
me at home," said Odysseus. But for
one whole year he stayed on Circe's
island.

Then one day he went to Circe and
said he must leave for home.

"It's such a dangerous voyage!" she
sobbed. "You must pass the singing
hideous sirens and then the whirlpool
Charybdis ... But if you must go, listen
carefully and do exactly as I tell you."

Circe told Odysseus and his men to

plug their ears with wax so as not to hear the song of the sirens. But Odysseus was curious to hear the famous singers. After setting sail, he told his men to rope him to the mast. And he did not plug his ears.

As the last knot of rope was tied, a sort of music came floating across the ocean.

"Circe lied. These sirens aren't hideous at all," thought Odysseus when an island came into view. "They're beautiful! Untie me, men, and let me swim over and speak to them!"

But his men could not hear him. The sirens' singing grew sweeter: its loveliness almost burst Odysseus' heart.

"Untie me!" he cried. "You go on, if you like, but I must stay. These ladies need me. Listen! They're calling me! Let me go!"

But his men could not hear him, and as the boat sailed away from the island, the singing grew softer.

"What did you see?" asked Odysseus.

"Vultures with women's heads, perched on a rock," said his friends. "And the bones of a thousand dead sailors."

Then Odysseus knew that Circe had not lied.

He also knew that a worse danger lay ahead: Charybdis.

Charybdis was more than a whirlpool. It was a great sucking mouth in the face of the ocean, in the shadow of a cliff. Twice a day it sucked in everything floating within seven miles of it. Twice a day it spewed out the wreckage. But thanks to Circe's advice, the men of Ithaca raced past Charybdis at the safest time of day and came to no harm at all.

But the sea god Poseidon's revenge was not over. His storm horses drove the *Odyssey* back, back, back, towards

that terrible gaping mouth. The soldiers
just had time to say goodbye to each
other before their ship slipped over the
glassy rim. For a moment it hung in
mid-air. Odysseus leapt on to the stern,

sprang upwards, and caught hold of a
little bush growing on the cliff. Down
fell his ship and men into the raging
whirlpool beneath.

For four aching hours Odysseus
clung to that bush, soaked with spray
and deafened by roaring water. Then
the tide filled Charybdis and stilled the
whirling water. Broken pieces of his

ship floated to the surface. Odysseus dropped down, clung to a plank of wood, and floated away across the sea.

For nine more years Odysseus had to travel the oceans from island to island, until at last he found help and friendship and a ship to carry him home to Ithaca.

Meanwhile Penelope waited patiently for her husband's return. Each day she watched at the window, but Odysseus did not come.

Others did. Idle, greedy young princes came calling on Penelope. "Odysseus must have drowned on his way home from the war," they said. "Marry one of us instead."

"I will wait a little longer," said Penelope politely.

But as the years passed, the visitors
became less charming. "Choose, lady,
or we will choose for you. Ithaca needs
a king."

"Very well," said Penelope at last.
"Let me weave a wedding veil. When
it's finished, I will choose a new
husband."

But although Penelope worked all day at her loom, the veil never seemed to be finished. Months passed and it had hardly grown at all. And why? Because every night, while her unwelcome suitors were snoring, Penelope crept out of bed and unpicked her needlework.

Then one night she was found out. One of the suitors found her at her loom, unpicking the threads by candlelight. "Enough!" he snarled. "Tomorrow you'll choose a husband, like it or not."

The ship bound for Ithaca with Odysseus aboard set sail while Poseidon was dozing. Imagine the sea god's fury when he woke and saw

Odysseus, his hated enemy, sleeping safe and sound on an Ithacan beach.

Poseidon punished the ship that had helped Odysseus reach home – seized it and cursed it into stone. There it stands, to this day, a narrow ship of rock with stone rowers bending over stony oars. The seagulls perch on it and shriek.

The day came when Penelope must choose a new husband from among the greedy princes. A great feast was arranged. But the unhappy queen ate none of the food laid in front of her. "If only he had come," she thought.

The suitors crammed their mouths and drank themselves drunk.

Outside in the yard lay an old dog –
Odysseus' old hunting dog. He got
nothing but kicks and cuffs from the
princes. His bones showed through his
dull coat, and his eyes were blind. Just
then, a ragged old beggar shuffled into
the yard and sat down. The dog raised

his head and sniffed – and got up and
tottered towards the sound of a
familiar voice.

"Hello, old friend. You remember
me, don't you?" The dog laid his head
in the beggar's lap and, content at last,
died with his head between loving
hands.

The beggar shuffled into the hall
where the feast was in progress. At one

chair after another he begged a bite of
food, a sup of wine. "I'm a poor unfor-
tunate sailor, shipwrecked on these
shores. Spare me a little something."

But the suitors drove him away with
slaps and kicks. Only Queen Penelope
asked him to eat
the food set in her
place. "Somewhere
on his journeys my
husband,
Odysseus, may
have asked for help
from strangers. I
hope he found at
least one heart to
pity him."

"Odysseus?" jeered the suitors. "He's dead and gone! Choose! It's time for you to choose one of us!" And they thumped the table. "Choose! Choose! Choose!"

"Very well." Penelope spoke with quiet dignity. "You shall compete for my hand. And this is the task I set. Put your axes on the table, head down. See how each one has a thong on its handle? Well, I shall marry the first man who can fire an arrow

directly through all those thongs ...
using the dead king's own bow."

The suitors swept the food off the
table. They snatched Odysseus' hunting
bow off the wall and struggled to string
it. But though they grunted and
strained, they could not bend the bow.

"Allow me," said the beggar, and bent it as though it were willow, and strung it. The suitors kicked him into a corner.

Then each tried to fire an arrow through the thongs of the axes. They all failed and cursed and argued. The axes tumbled a hundred times.

Penelope got up to leave the hall.

"May I try?" asked the beggar.

"Get away you filthy creature," said a prince. "This contest is for the hand of a queen!"

"Let him try," said Penelope. "I'd as soon marry a penniless beggar as any one of you." And she closed the door behind her.

But once the beggar had the bow in his hands, he did not take aim on the axes. He leapt on to the table and fired one arrow after another – into the hearts of the suitors.

"Hear this and die!" he shouted. "Odysseus has returned to rid his palace of rats and toads!"

Penelope heard the fighting and thought the suitors must be quarrelling again. At last, silence. Her son came running to find her. "He's outside! He's killed them all, Mother! He's home! After all these years, Father has come home!"

Penelope went down to the hall. There stood Odysseus, his disguise thrown off and his face washed. "Welcome, sir," she said rather coldly. "You must be weary. I'll have a bed made up for you."

Odysseus' heart sank. Had Penelope's

love died during the twenty years he
had been away? "I'd rather sleep in my
own bed, lady," he said timidly.

"Very well. I shall have it carried to
the east chamber."

A spark twinkled in Odysseus' eye.
"How could you move our bed when
it's carved out of the very tree which
holds up the roof of this palace?"

When Penelope heard his words, she fell into Odysseus' arms and kissed him. "I had to be sure it was you. And only you could know about our bed!" she said. "Welcome home, Odysseus!"